MUMMIES, TEMPLES
AND TOMBS

An imprint of HarperCollins*Publishers*

Mummies, Temples and Tombs accompanies the television series *Ancient Egyptians* created by Wall to Wall for Channel Four, TLC ® and Granada International in association with Canal+, Norddeutscher Rundfunk/Germany, RAI – Radiotelevisione Italiana, Seven Network Australia and Warner Home Video Inc., A Warner Bros. Entertainment Company.

First published in Great Britain by HarperCollins*Publishers* Ltd in 2003
Text copyright © 2003 HarperCollins*Publishers* Ltd,
77-85 Fulham Palace Road, Hammersmith, London W6 8JB
Front cover photograph by Giles Keyte © Wall to Wall (Egypt) Ltd 2002

wall to wall

The Wall to Wall website address is: www.walltowall.co.uk

The HarperCollins website address is: www.harpercollins.co.uk

1 3 5 7 9 10 8 6 4 2
ISBN 0 00 715378 3

Designer: Elorine Grant
Cover Designer: James Annal
Illustrator: Tim Stevens
Editor: Terry Vittachi
Consultant: Dr Ian Shaw

Printed and bound in Great Britain by Clays Ltd, St Ives plc

Contents

 INTRODUCTION

Mummies, Temples and Tombs tells the stories of five real Egyptians who lived between 2350 and 4250 years ago. Not all of them were rich and powerful. One of the stories is about a fourteen-year-old weaver named Nakht. He came from a poor family and, because of a misunderstanding at the temple where he worked, he found himself sent to do hard work in the quarries where stone used in temples and tombs was found.

These people lived at different times in Egyptian history. When Weni was alive, Egypt was powerful and well respected by other countries. Things were very different when Nectanebo II was Pharaoh, nearly 2000 years later. By then, Egypt had lost much of its power and was threatened by powerful enemies. Although Nectanebo was the last Egyptian Pharaoh, he was able to use a secret power that all the Pharaohs before him had used, and this protected Egypt from invasion for sixteen years.

Seven hundred years earlier, Wenamun had discovered that the power of Egypt was no longer respected in other countries. He was sent on a long voyage to collect precious wood for use in the temple at Karnak, and the story of his journey tells of the hardships and risks he had to face.

Thutmose was what we would call a sculptor. When he was alive, 3300 years ago, carving stone was a craft practised by different kinds of workers in temples and tombs. Thutmose, however, was one of the most creative craftsmen of his time, and we know about him because of his studio and the wonderful works of art that were found in them, which include a famous carved portrait of the Egyptian queen named Nefertiti.

The stories of these five real Egyptians help us to understand the world they inhabited and how they lived their lives. Finding out about them helps to bring us closer to other people, times and places from way back in history.

CHAPTER ONE

THE PLOT TO KILL THE KING

A story from 4250 years ago

Main characters in the story:

Weni (*When-ee*) – *a palace official*

Iww (*Yoo-woo*) – *court vizier to Teti and father of Weni*

Pepi (*Pep-ee*) – *king of Egypt and friend of Weni*

King Teti (*Tet-ee*) – *father of Pepi*

King Merenre (*Mur-en-ray*) – *son of Pepi*

Weretyamtes (*Weh-ret-yam-tez*) – *wife of Pepi*

Mereruka (*Meh-re-roo-ka*) – *court vizier to Pepi*

Nebet (*Neb-ette*) – *a harem attendant*

Userkare (*Yoo-sir-car-ray*) – *briefly king of Egypt*

INTRODUCTION

WHEN WENI WAS AN OLD MAN he could look back at his life and feel proud of what he had achieved. He had still been young when he had been given the job of running the royal estates, which supplied food and workers for the king, his family and all the other people in the royal household. Weni had been a general as well. Five times he had led the army into battle against the Sand Dwellers when they tried to rebel against Egypt. Weni had collected taxes for the king and had organized the building of the king's pyramid.

For all this Weni had been richly rewarded. The king had given him permission to use special Tura limestone to build his own tomb. This was a great honour for Weni, who understood better than most people what it meant. His fine tomb would not only show people how powerful and important he was while he was alive, but long after he had died people would still know that Weni had become one of the most important people in the kingdom.

Yes, Weni had much to be proud of. Three kings had reigned over Egypt during his lifetime. Weni had known them all well: King Teti, King Pepi and King Merenre. But his closest friend of the three was Pepi, and it was for him that Weni had carried out his most important and most secret task – a task that would save the king's life. Even when he was an old man and knew that it would not be long before he would be laid to rest for ever in his magnificent tomb, Weni remembered clearly how he had uncovered the plot to kill the king.

PART ONE

Friends in high places

WENI'S FRIENDSHIP WITH PEPI reached back to the time when they were little boys. Like all the king's children, Pepi had been brought up in the part of the king's household called the royal harem. Although the harem was in the royal palace, it was a private area where the queens and the royal children lived. In some ways the royal harem was like a little kingdom all of its own. It had its own attendants, who worked in the harem alone and not in any other part of the palace. The harem had its own land, its own cattle, its own grain mills and its own workshops where material was woven. These gave the royal harem its own wealth and made it independent of the palace and the government.

Although the harem was a special place belonging to the king, the king's children were not the only ones brought up there. Certain children from other powerful families were allowed to grow up there as well, and one of these children was Weni. His father, called Iww, had been the vizier, the most important official in the kingdom and second in power only to the king himself. When Weni was born, King Teti had allowed Iww's little son to join the royal harem. This was a great honour for Iww. For Weni it was the first step on his own rise to power and fame.

Life in the harem

LIVING IN THE HAREM gave Weni the best of everything. There was always plenty to eat, and not only bread and beer, which most people in Egypt ate and drank. From the harem farms there were supplies of fresh fruit and vegetables: beans, onions, figs, dates and melons. The farms also sent milk, sheep, goats and pigs to the harem. Then there were those special delicacies which only the rich could afford: beef, game birds, rare and delicious meats like antelope and, of course, wine. Living in the harem gave Weni a taste for the best things in life.

Unlike most people in Egypt, Weni grew up surrounded by furniture – another privilege of the rich. All through the royal palace, visitors would be amazed at the sight of elegant chairs and tables made from wood and inlaid with gold and other precious metals. There were beds in the palace, too, comforts unknown to most of the king's subjects.

The rooms in the harem were clean and spacious. Ordinary people lived in small houses made of mud bricks, which many of them shared with the animals they kept. These smelly, dusty hovels were very different to the comfortable surroundings in which Weni grew up. Harem servants swept the floors clean.

The walls were decorated with colourful pictures. Weni and the other children could play in the tree-lined gardens, and most of all they could wash as often as the queens and other ladies who also lived in the harem. Staying clean became second nature to Weni from an early age.

As a little boy Weni rarely wore clothes, and when he was older, he would dress in a neatly pleated kilt, which was all that was needed in the hot climate of Egypt. However, Weni could see all round him the care that the queens and other harem ladies took over their appearance. After bathing, their bodies would be massaged, softened and perfumed. Black kohl was used to paint their eyebrows, outline their eyes and darken their eyelashes. They wore different wigs for different occasions. But it was their jewellery that Weni remembered most from his early childhood. Bright and glittering, he was fascinated by the flashing of gold and precious stones as they caught the light. He remembered the rustle of necklaces made from rows and rows of beads and jewels. And whenever an elegant hand reached out to him, it was followed by the tinkle of bangles and bracelets.

Everyday life for the court

LIFE IN THE ROYAL HAREM may have been more comfortable than life in the world outside the palace walls, but there was still work to be done. Many of the women in the harem spun and wove different types of material used in the palace for clothing and furnishings. Other women served as dancers and singers. Some were entertainers at the splendid feasts given by the king. Some performed sacred dances and sang in the temple.

Weni and the other children had work of their own too. As soon as they were old enough they began school lessons. Most Egyptian children learned to do what their parents did. So the sons of farmers learned about farming, the sons of fishermen learned how to catch fish, the sons of bakers learned how to make bread and the sons of craftsmen learned a craft like carpentry or working with metal. Girls were expected to be able to look after a family, so they learned from their mothers how to cook and run a household.

Weni and boys like him, the sons of the men who ran the country, had to learn the skills needed to govern a nation like Egypt. In their lessons they learned to read and write. They studied mathematics. Religion was an important part of their schooling. Some boys learned medicine, some were taught the building and engineering skills needed for large construction work, such as building a pyramid. Lessons in the royal palace could be just as hard and the teachers just as fierce as lessons and teachers in other Egyptian schools. Weni studied well and learned quickly, yet he did not escape a beating when he made a mistake in his school work. The same went for his friend Pepi, even though Pepi was the king's son.

One day Pepi would inherit his father's role as Pharaoh. He would need to be a warrior, but he would also need to be learned and wise.

PART TWO

Religion and rumours

OF COURSE, as Weni used to remind himself, his life in the royal harem had one important difference to that of the life of other boys his age, even the ones who came from families rich enough to send them to school. Living in the palace, Weni lived in the house of the king, and to every Egyptian the king was also a god. So Weni grew up in the home of both his god and his king.

The religious beliefs of King Teti were different to those of the kings who had reigned in Egypt before him. Earlier kings had been loyal to the sun-god, Re, but King Teti had broken the tradition and many people in the kingdom were angry at what he had done. In secret they still worshipped Re as the most important of their gods, and as Weni grew older he became aware of this unease: even in the palace there were rumours about the king and the old religious beliefs he had replaced.

Under King Teti, Weni was given his first official post in the palace when he was made sandal-bearer. The king's vizier was Mereruka and, like all the king's officials, Weni had to obey Mereruka's orders. Now he was a royal sandal-bearer Weni began to mix with the king's most important officials as well as with members of the royal family, like Pepi. He began to notice some people in the palace whispering in small groups. The king seemed to grow nervous. His bodyguards stayed closer to him than ever. In fact, whenever Weni saw the king he noticed that his bodyguards were always with him.

The unthinkable crime

WHEN HE WAS AN OLD MAN Weni still remembered those far-off days of his youth. Perhaps he should have seen what was coming. But he was still young. How could he have understood what was going on in secret behind the king's back?

And then it had happened – the unthinkable. King Teti was murdered. Weni was at his lessons in the temple when servants from the royal harem burst in looking for Pepi. Through the open door came the sound of shouting and feet running up and down the cool, shady corridors and passages. But inside the schoolroom everything was still and quiet as if time itself had stopped.

'What's the matter?' Pepi asked the head servant.

The man tried to speak, but the words seemed to stick in his mouth. Then one of the others blurted out, 'Your royal father has been murdered. Save yourself, sir.'

'Murdered?' said Pepi, turning pale and dropping his writing brush. 'By whom?'

'By his bodyguards,' said the head servant, finding his voice at last. 'Quickly, your highness. You must come with us. Back to the safety of the harem.'

It seemed like a dream. Everything happened in a blur. Weni left his writing board lying on the schoolroom floor. Pepi knocked over his ink in his haste to leave. Surrounded by harem servants, they hurried away down small passages set back from the main parts of the palace until they reached the harem, and the heavy doors were barred shut behind them.

Here, for a while, they were safe. But Weni would always remember the feeling of fear that settled over the harem like a chill mist from the river. Outside the high walls shouts and screams echoed through the royal palace. They could hear soldiers marching and from the temple cries of 'Re. . . Re. . . Re' rose up to heaven from the followers of the sun-god. That was the moment when Weni understood what had happened. King Teti had been murdered because he had turned against the sun-god and now the followers of the god Re had taken their revenge. Would anyone in the royal household now be safe? These were dangerous times – times that Weni never forgot.

A time of mourning and a time of danger

ACCORDING TO TRADITION, when a king died all Egypt went into mourning. People tore their clothes and plastered their heads with mud. No one ate meat. No one drank wine. No one slept on comfortable beds. No one took a bath or used perfume. For seventy days they mourned King Teti, and after this came the royal funeral when his body was laid to rest.

This was a dangerous time for Pepi in particular. As the eldest son of the dead king it was his duty to make offerings in the temple dedicated to the memory of his father. According to tradition Pepi should also have succeeded his father as king. But the followers of the sun-god had plans of their own. They wanted to restore Re as the most important of the gods. To do this they needed a king who believed in Re above all other gods. For this reason, a man named Userkare was at first made king instead of Pepi. The last part of his name, –re, contained the name of the sun-god, proving that Userkare was a loyal follower.

Pepi had supporters of his own, however: people who had served his father and who wanted to see King Teti's son continue his work as king. Pepi had been patient and careful. He had watched and waited, seeing how Userkare set about his rule. Pepi did not have to wait long. Userkare may have been a faithful follower of the sun-god in heaven, but on earth, in Egypt, he no longer had the power of the early kings who had followed Re. He had reigned for no longer than a year when he was removed from the throne and King Teti's son was made ruler over Egypt, beginning his long reign as King Pepi I.

PART THREE

A new rule in Egypt

WHEN PEPI BECAME KING OF EGYPT, it marked the beginning of Weni's own rise to power. Early in his reign, the new king promoted his childhood friend to the very important post of 'Sole Companion'. This showed all Egypt that Weni had a very close personal connection with the king. From now on Weni would escort King Pepi in victory celebrations, military parades and royal hunts. Now that he was 'Sole Companion' to the king, Weni became King Pepi's most trusted adviser as well as his closest friend. This was important for Weni and, as it turned out, it was very important for King Pepi as well.

King Pepi had a royal harem like his father King Teti and many kings before him. This harem was very similar to the one in which Weni had grown up. Weni understood the customs of life in the harem and he also understood how people in the harem could plan and organize things in secrecy without other people in the palace knowing what they were doing. Of all King Pepi's servants and officials, Weni probably knew as much about a royal harem as the king himself. Perhaps this was the reason why one of the ladies in the royal harem told him about a terrible secret she had uncovered.

The lady was called Nebet. Like Weni, she came from a noble family, and like him she had grown up with a close understanding of life in the harem. Nebet would help the queen with important personal tasks, such as taking her daily bath, dressing, putting on her make-up, choosing which wig to wear and selecting her jewellery. Other duties of harem women might include playing board games with the queen. They walked in the palace gardens, dined together and attended the great royal feasts held in the palace. Indeed, Nebet may have been as close to the queen, Weretyamtes, as Weni was to the queen's husband, King Pepi.

Secrets and suspicions

PEOPLE IN THE HAREM had plenty of time to talk to each other. They talked about their friends, and about people they liked and didn't like. They talked about life in the palace and people in the government. There was always plenty of time for talking in the harem, and sometimes people overheard things they were not meant to hear. This is what happened to Nebet.

One day she was passing through the harem when she overheard Queen Weretyamtes and a group of other harem ladies talking. The queen sounded angry. Nebet could not hear clearly what she was saying, but she did hear the queen speaking about her husband, King Pepi. Then she heard the queen laugh angrily and tell her friends she did not know how much longer he would be king in Egypt. 'Perhaps King Pepi will have an accident, like his father,' the queen said. 'Perhaps people closest to him think the time has come for him to join the gods in heaven.'

Nebet felt her heart beating fast when she heard what the queen had said. Quickly she looked round to see if anyone else had overheard. But Nebet was alone and out of sight of the queen and the ladies she was talking to. Only Nebet knew what the queen had been talking about. Who could she turn to? How could she warn the king? No wonder she felt scared. The queen was very powerful, especially in the harem. If she knew that Nebet had discovered what she had been saying she could have had the lady punished, taken from the harem or even killed. Nebet knew this all too well. She needed someone powerful to help her, but not someone who lived in the harem. That was why she chose to tell the king's 'Sole Companion', his childhood friend Weni.

Dangerous talk

WHEN NEBET CAME TO WENI with her awful secret, she was pale and frightened. 'I must speak to you in private,' she told him. 'What I have to say, I can only say to you alone.'

Weni could see she was trembling and he took her to a private chamber, where she could speak in safety.

'Please understand me when I tell you that my life is at risk,' she began. Weni looked serious and poured her a cup of wine to help calm her nerves.

'I will protect you,' he told Nebet. 'Whatever it is you have to say, I will protect you. So tell me what it is that makes you so scared.'

'I am frightened for the king,' she told him. 'I am frightened that someone close to the king may try to hurt him.'

'Hurt him?' asked Weni. 'How do you mean, hurt him?'

'I think someone may be planning to kill the king,' Nebet said.

'Kill the king,' Weni repeated slowly, letting the words sink into his mind. 'Do you know who this is?'

'Yes, I do, and that is why I am afraid.'

Weni looked at the woman's face and her large frightened eyes. 'You said that it is someone close to the king.' Nebet nodded her head. 'Is it someone in the harem? Someone close to the king in the harem?' Again Nebet nodded her head.

Weni smiled and nodded his own head. Now he understood why Nebet was scared. Now he understood who was plotting against the king.

'Thank you for telling me,' he told the frightened woman. 'Your secret is safe, and thanks to you we still have time to stop any harm coming to the king. Now, go back to the harem and try to carry on as if nothing has happened.'

Nebet felt better after this. She remembered what had happened to King Teti, and she had taken a great risk in trying to save his son from being murdered in the same way. At least her secret was shared with the king's Sole Companion. If anyone could stop the plotters, the king's old friend could.

PART FOUR

Whispers and lies

THE NEXT TIME NEBET SAW WENI was in the harem. He didn't come with soldiers, or with lawyers or palace officials. Weni came alone, as if he was paying a visit to old friends. What Nebet did not know was that the king had sent Weni to the harem to uncover the plot and punish those who were planning to murder him.

The women who had looked after Weni when he was a child in the harem were old now and they were always happy to see him. On this visit Nebet watched him talking to them for a long time, listening to their news and laughing with them as they remembered their happy times together. Then she saw Weni leave the group of old women and make his way towards one of the queen's close friends.

Nebet watched Weni lead this lady away from the crowd into a quiet chamber of the harem. A little time later the lady appeared alone and Nebet could see that she was pale and had a worried look on her face. Nebet saw her whisper to another of the queen's friends, who looked round nervously and then whispered back her reply. They were still talking to each other in hushed voices when Weni appeared behind them and spoke in a whisper as well.

Meanwhile the queen was laughing and talking with other friends seated around a pool in the harem gardens. That was where she was sitting when the crowd round her moved aside to let Weni approach her. The laughing and talking died away as the king's Sole Companion stood in front of Queen Weretyamtes and asked her, 'Your Majesty, may I speak to you in private?'

The queen smiled and answered, 'Of course you may. Ladies, would you leave us alone, please. My friend, Weni, has a very serious look today. He must have something important to tell me.'

Nebet saw the other ladies move away from Weni and the queen. Some went deeper into the gardens. Some went to their rooms. One found her musical instrument and started playing a tune. Nebet thought the music sounded sad as it drifted through the tall cool halls and chambers of the harem.

A plot uncovered

WENI SAT BESIDE THE QUEEN and began talking. Nebet could not hear what he said. Side by side, they looked as if they were old friends enjoying a chat. But Nebet could see the laughter and happiness disappear from the queen's face as Weni spoke. At first the queen tried to answer back, but Weni stopped her until he had finished speaking. And when he finished, the queen lowered her head and had nothing to say. Nebet watched her wipe tears from her eyes and look at Weni, but Weni's face was as cold and firm as stone. The queen laid her hand on Weni's arm and tried to tell him something, but Weni got to his feet and walked away without looking back. He gave a little nod to Nebet as he passed her. It looked like a nod of greeting, but Nebet knew what it really meant: the plot to kill the king had been uncovered and King Pepi had been saved.

Nebet never discovered if the queen herself was plotting to kill the king. Maybe she was giving information about her husband to someone else planning to murder him. Whatever she was doing, it threatened both her king and her god. Weretyamtes lost her power in the harem. The friends who had once crowded round her now stayed away from her. So did King Pepi. His queen had betrayed him. She had plotted with others to murder him and now it was her turn to fear for her life.

Rewards and punishments

HOWEVER, ONE LADY IN THE HAREM did benefit from the plot to kill the king. After her brave action, Nebet won Pepi's trust. In time King Pepi married two new wives and they were the daughters of Nebet. These daughters gave birth to two sons who would both become kings of Egypt: King Merenre and his younger brother King Pepi II.

Weni too had shown his loyalty to the king. He had also shown his old friend that he knew how to take care of secret plots in the palace. When Nebet had come to Weni with her terrible secret, he did not know how many people were plotting with the queen, or how powerful they were. All he did know was that he had to act carefully and quietly. He had to be cautious. It was important that he did not arouse suspicion or make the plotter think he knew what they were doing.

That was why Weni had gone to the harem alone and spoken to his old friends from his childhood. From them he had heard enough to understand what had been going on. When he had spoken quietly to the queen's close friends, it seemed to them that Weni knew all about the plot, even though he only knew part of their secret plans. The queen's friends had told him the rest. They had given him the information he needed to show Weretyamtes that he knew there was a plot against the king. After that, it had been easy. The officials plotting with her were punished.

The names of the guilty men were scratched off their tombs and any other carvings. In time they were forgotten, unlike Weni. He faithfully served King Pepi I and his son King Merenre for many years to come, and when he died and was laid to rest he knew that thousands of years later people would still read and understand that he had saved the life of his king

CHAPTER TWO

THE LOST TREASURES OF THE ROYAL SCULPTOR

A story from 3334 years ago

Main characters in the story:

Thutmose (*Thoot-mows*) – *a sculptor*

Akhenaten (*Akk-en-nart-ten*) – *Pharaoh of Egypt*

Nefertiti (*Neff-ur-teet-ee*) – *queen of Egypt*

Meritaten (*Meh-rit-ah-ten*) – *daughter of Akhenaten and Nefertiti*

Meketaten (*Meh-ket-aah-ten*) – *another daughter of the Pharaoh and his queen*

Tutankhamun (*Toot-ank-ah-men*) – *the next Pharaoh of Egypt*

Ramose (*Ra-mose-ay*) – *a general*

Nakhte (*Nak-t*) – *the court vizier*

Panehsy (*Pah-nech-see*) *and* **Pawah (*Pa-wach*)** –
priests in the temple

INTRODUCTION

AT SOME TIME in their lives most little boys want to be like their fathers. Thutmose certainly did. His father was a skilled craftsman who could cut pictures in rock and copy inscriptions in hieroglyphs, which even then people knew would last for thousands of years. That was why so much time and care was taken over the work that decorated the walls of temples and tombs in ancient Egypt. Here powerful people would be laid to rest when they ended their time on earth and entered the afterlife.

Craftsmen like Thutmose's father would spend months and months steadily working at the bare rock to create the decorated chamber where a nobleman or courtier, sometimes the Pharaoh himself, would pass from this world to the next. The craftsmen worked as a team. Some, such as Thutmose's father, would chip at the rock with heavy stone hammers and sharp tools made of bronze. It was their job to cut out the basic shape of a picture or an inscription. When they had finished, other craftsmen took over polishing the designs with smoothing stones and powders which they used like sandpaper. The final craftsmen to get to work were the painters, who brought the designs to life with bright, exciting colours.

Watching over their work would be the draughtsman who

had drawn up the original design on papyrus. He needed to check that the men chiselling the outline shapes were following his design accurately. If a problem arose, if they came to a natural crack in the rock for instance, the craftsmen and designer would decide together the best way to get round it.

Thutmose remembered well what his father had told him, 'Think twice and chip once when you are carving rock – because you can chip it out much more easily than you can stick it back!' And Thutmose's father made very few mistakes in his work. That was why he was respected by all the designers and craftsmen he worked with. That was why Thutmose had wanted to be like him.

Thutmose's father had died before his son had created his most famous work. Even so, the old man knew that one day Thutmose would show that he had an even greater skill in working with stone than his own.

PART ONE

Pharaoh's favourite sculptor

LIFE WAS GOOD FOR THUTMOSE. His special skill had made him well known. It had made him rich as well. He owned a fine house in a smart area of the royal city of Akhetaten. Thutmose had his own chariot and stable of horses to carry him about its streets and on his travels around the surrounding area.

Perhaps most important of all, he was a favourite sculptor of the Pharaoh, Akhenaten, and his queen, Nefertiti. Yes, life was good for Thutmose. At least, life had been good while Akhenaten had been alive. Now he was dead and Egypt had a new Pharaoh, Thutmose was not so sure. Many big changes had been made during Akhenaten's reign and now it looked as if the country was about to suffer even bigger changes.

Changes made people worried and it was because of worries about the future that Thutmose had taken the most important decision of his life. In spite of the wealth and success he had enjoyed in the city of Akhetaten, he was going to leave – to pack away his unfinished work, close up his studio and return to the old capital of Thebes. Thutmose was not alone. Many of his neighbours, rich important people like him, were doing the same. He did not know what would become of the city Akhetaten after he and so many other people had gone. Perhaps he would return one day, but he couldn't be sure. No one seemed sure of anything now that Akhenaten was no longer Pharaoh.

Changing times

THERE WAS AN EERIE SILENCE in his studio when Thutmose opened the door and entered for the last time. In the past the street outside had been full of bustle and business. Merchants used to hurry past with food and other goods they wanted to sell in the market. There used to be the happy sounds of children playing in the streets. Sometimes the clip-clop of horses' hooves and crunch of chariot wheels let

Thutmose know that one of his neighbours was on the move: Ramose the general, most likely, or Nakhte the vizier. They owned splendid villas nearby, with stone doorways at the entrance in which their names had been carved. When Thutmose was working in his studio other friends like Panehsy and Pawah, priests in the great temple, would often drop in to pass the time of day.

But Panehsy and Pawah had already packed up their houses and moved away. Thutmose wasn't sure where they were living now. Ramose and Nakhte would be leaving soon, they told him. The court of the new Pharaoh was moving back to the old capital, so they would be going there as well. The royal city of Akhetaten had grown out of the desert beside the river Nile only twelve years earlier. Thutmose and his family had been happy there; he would be sorry to say goodbye to it. But he was a craftsman like his father and his father before him and craftsmen had to move to where they could find work. For twelve years Thutmose had found good work in Akhetaten. Now that work was over, finished for a long time to come as far as he could see. He had to look for work in a different place – back in the old capital at Thebes.

Unfinished business

INSIDE THE STUDIO, Thutmose closed the door behind him and looked around to see what needed to be done before he left for the last time. Usually the room would be noisy with the sound of his apprentices who were studying how to work in stone. Other craftsmen had been here alongside Thutmose, stone polishers and painters like the ones who worked on the walls of temples and tombs. They were gone now, taking their tools with them, leaving their work on the benches, half-finished, awaiting the next stage of completion.

There were more than twenty plaster casts of clay models of people's heads: portraits that Thutmose and his fellow craftsmen had been asked to create for rich clients. There were other sculptures in different kinds of stone, both hard stone and soft stone. Some of these sculptures had only recently been started; you could just make out the rough outline of a person's head and face chipped into the stone, but weeks and weeks of work would be needed to complete the finished piece. Other sculptures had been rubbed smooth and polished and were only waiting for the painter to bring them to life with colour.

PART TWO

The face of a queen

THUTMOSE MOVED AROUND THE STUDIO, touching the pieces one by one, recalling in his mind the workmen who had been carefully shaping it. There was one piece that he saved until last. The work on it was completed, the paint was dry. It was ready to be delivered to the client who was paying for it, but Thutmose wondered if this client would ever see the beautiful sculpture he was now looking at on his own bench.

It was not only the sculpture itself that was beautiful – the craftsmanship was superb. Thutmose was proud to call it his own. But the person it represented, the woman whose portrait it was, was beautiful as well. She was Akhenaten's queen, Nefertiti. Alone in the studio, gazing at the sculpture in front of him, Thutmose could almost imagine that the queen herself was there with him. It felt as if she was looking back approvingly at the craftsman who had created this perfect image of her. The craftsman and the queen both hoped it would show people what she looked like for long into the future.

This sculpture of the queen was unlike many other carvings of her and the Pharaoh. These other carvings made their bodies look different, with long, stretched heads and swollen tummies. It was part of a new artistic style that the Pharaoh liked. Some people said that the Pharaoh himself showed his designers and craftsmen how he wanted them to carve himself and the queen in this new style. For Thutmose, who knew the Pharaoh and his queen well, this way of showing them was an important example of the changes that had taken place while Akhenaten was Pharaoh.

A new god

THE PHARAOH had not been called Akhenaten when he had become Pharaoh. At that time his name had been Amenhotep.

However, Amenhotep and his wife Nefertiti had a daughter called Meritaten, whose name meant 'Beloved of Aten'. The Aten was a new kind of god. Its worshippers believed that the Aten was the creator of the universe. The Aten was best described as being like the golden disc of the sun that moved daily across the sky.

When Prince Amenhotep named his baby daughter after the Aten, it was clear that he himself was a worshipper of the Aten. So few people were surprised when, after reigning as Pharaoh for four or five years, he changed his name to show his people that he believed in the Aten. That was how Amenhotep became Akhenaten: adding the name of the god to the end of his own name.

Akhenaten took his new name four or five years after becoming Pharaoh. By that time it was clear that the new Pharaoh not only worshipped the Aten, but he had also abandoned most of the traditional gods that had been worshipped in Egypt for centuries. This came as a terrible shock to believers in the old gods. In particular it was a shock to the priests of the god Amun in the great temple at Karnak. They had grown rich and powerful over hundreds and hundreds of years. Now the Pharaoh was taking power from them by worshipping the Aten as the new god of Egypt.

It was not only the priests who saw their world being turned upside down. Throughout the royal city of Thebes rumours started spreading that the Pharaoh wanted to build a new city devoted to the Aten. If this happened, Thebes would no longer be the most important city in the land.

The Temple of the Aten

THE RUMOURS PROVED TO BE TRUE. In the sixth year of his reign the young Pharaoh sailed away to the north, following the River Nile in search of a place where he could build a new city devoted to the Aten. Akhenaten's royal ship had sailed for three hundred and seventy kilometres when he came to a place on the east bank of the river where he found a plain encircled by cliffs.

The plain was deserted and the next morning the Pharaoh went ashore and rode around to explore the site. It did not take him long to make up his mind that this was the place where he should build his new city. He called it Akhetaten, meaning 'The Horizon of the Aten' and he ordered building work to begin right away.

The city, which grew quickly from the desert plain, was dominated by the Great Temple of the Aten. This was different from the temples to other Egyptian gods like Amun. The Great Temple of the Aten was a huge open courtyard filled with stone altar tables at which everyone could make offerings of fresh food and drink every day to the god.

Close to the Great Temple was the royal palace. The Royal Road ran right through the middle of it, dividing the palace into two parts. These were joined by a bridge on which the royal family could often be seen crossing from one side of the palace to the other.

The changes Akhenaten was making were to touch all aspects of life in Egypt. There was a new god, a new city, and a new style of art which sculptors like Thutmose would have to follow.

PART THREE

A new style of painting

NORTH AND SOUTH OF THE GREAT TEMPLE and the royal palace lay the suburbs where the chief courtiers and other rich people, like Thutmose, had built their houses. Many of these had gardens with pools surrounded by trees. They also had their own kitchen blocks and private bathrooms.

The curving cliffs which lay to the east of the new city became the site of tombs cut into the rock for many of the courtiers, and it was here that Thutmose spent much of his working time. When he had worked on tombs, Thutmose's father had been ordered to follow a very strict style that was meant to show and describe the owner of the tomb in the afterlife.

However, the tombs that Thutmose decorated at Akhetaten were very different. The Pharaoh, Akhenaten, wanted tomb decorations to show life around the city. So Thutmose and craftsmen like him found themselves creating pictures and descriptions of houses, temples and palaces that they knew well. They created lifelike pictures of birds and animals. And they showed real people living real lives. This was very different to the sort of tomb decoration that had gone before, especially when it showed the royal family behaving like every other family in the kingdom. There were pictures of Akhenaten and Nefertiti playing with their little daughters, the royal princesses. In one picture the Pharaoh was shown holding a baby daughter in his arms, giving her a tender kiss. These were everyday scenes that people knew from their own family lives, but to see official pictures of the king and queen behaving like this was new and different. Throughout the city, craftsmen like Thutmose were busy carving pictures of daily life. When they showed the royal family riding freely through the city, that was exactly what they did: the Pharaoh and his family moved among the citizens of Akhetaten, in the same easy way as their courtiers and officials and important subjects like Thutmose.

Looking at the portrait of Nefertiti in his studio, Thutmose remembered the hours that he had spent in her company while he had been working on it. There was something special about this queen, he felt. It seemed that she was almost an equal of her husband in ruling the country. She was beautiful and she was also wise and powerful. She must have worshipped the Aten as faithfully as her husband. However, there were some people in the kingdom who thought that the Pharaoh was spending too much time showing his devotion to the Aten and not spending enough time looking after his kingdom.

Thutmose's neighbour Ramose, a general in the army, had his doubts. He knew that the lands governed for the Pharaoh by the princes of the north were being attacked by the armies of the powerful Hittite empire. Time after time the princes had asked Egypt for help. They had sent tribute to Egypt. They had been loyal and faithful. Now they begged the Pharaoh to help them in return. They asked for soldiers and they asked for military aid to drive back their attackers. But, as Ramose told Thutmose, no soldiers and no help were ever sent from Egypt to help the princes in the north. The Pharaoh, it seemed, really was more interested in the realm of the Aten than in his own realm on earth. There was danger in this, Ramose had warned. If the Pharaoh ignored what was happening on the frontiers of the empire, Egypt's enemies would begin to close in and the power that Egypt had wielded for centuries would slowly slip away.

There were many changes taking place in Egypt, Thutmose had thought to himself, but how many of them were for the good? He wished he knew the answer. But these were answers only the gods knew. For Thutmose the big question was which god had the right answer: the traditional gods of Egypt like Amun, or the new power in the heavens – the Aten.

Fashioning a life

STILL, WHILE THE PHARAOH AND HIS QUEEN PAID Thutmose and other craftsmen to decorate their new city, Thutmose could not complain. All craftsmen in Egypt who made sculptures of people believed that they were creating a figure which would be able to come to life in the world where people went after they had died on earth. In fact the Egyptian word for a sculptor meant 'a fashioner of life'. A statue or a portrait was meant to follow the person it represented into the afterlife. It was a sort of stone twin, which could be brought to life when the right religious ritual was performed. This was why a person's name and official titles were chiselled into the base or back of a statue. This was how sculptures had been prepared in

Egypt for hundreds and hundreds of years. And that was why most of them were made in the same style and followed traditional designs.

Now that Akhenaten was Pharaoh, things were different. Thutmose still believed that the statues and sculptures he created were capable of coming to life. But he probably had even greater faith that this could happen because the Pharaoh encouraged him to make his work look so lifelike. Thutmose could clearly remember the sadness and misery that Akhenaten and Nefertiti had suffered when the second of their daughters had died. She had been called Meketaten and her father and mother had wept openly when she had been laid to rest in her tomb. Unlike other royal families in days gone by, this sad scene had been recorded, so that no one would ever forget it. On the wall of the princess's tomb was a carving showing the Pharaoh and his queen crying over their daughter's body. This was something real, something pictured and remembered for ever. That was what the Pharaoh and Nefertiti had wanted and that was what made Thutmose feel pleased and proud to work for them. He often wondered what his father would have made of this new realistic style. Thutmose hoped he would have approved.

Thutmose sat in the silent studio gazing at the portrait of Nefertiti, wondering how long it would be before he saw it again. It had been carved from a single block of limestone, which had then been painted in careful detail. What pleased him most were the queen's eyes. Holes shaped like human eyes had been hollowed from the stone face and into them had been set curved quartz crystals. These were held in place by a waxy glue which dried to a round black disc. Seen together, the clear rounded crystal and the black blob of glue behind it looked just like a human eye with a dark pupil. It was very realistic.

PART FOUR

A queen's grief

THE QUEEN'S FACE LOOKED CALM and confident in the stone carving. That was how Thutmose liked to remember her. She had looked very different a few months earlier when she had attended the burial of Akhenaten. The Pharaoh had died in his seventeenth year as king. He had been buried in his royal tomb set deep in a valley that ran into the cliffs on the east of the city. In the royal tomb there were side rooms made ready for the burials of the six princesses, daughters of Akhenaten and Nefertiti. Beyond these lay two corridors leading to the two principal burial chambers. These were the same size. In one of them Akhenaten was laid to rest. The other chamber had been prepared for Nefertiti. In death, as in life, she and Akhenaten would remain together for eternity.

Thutmose had watched the funeral procession. He had seen Nefertiti crying for her dead husband just as she had cried openly for their daughter Meketaten. But Thutmose knew that she was crying for more than the dead Pharaoh. When Akhenaten died there were many people in Egypt, powerful officials and priests, who wanted to return to the old ways and the old gods. They did not want to follow the Aten. They did not want to make Akhenaten the main city in Egypt. Now that the Pharaoh was dead, they saw their chance to return to the traditions of the past. Nefertiti knew that this could happen, and it made her very sad.

It was only a short time after Akhenaten had died that people began to change things back to the way they had been. The priests of the Temple of Amun at Karnak began to worship their god once again. Officials in the government, rich merchants and generals in the army closed up their homes in Akhetaten and returned up the river to the old capital at Thebes. Nefertiti also left the city she and her husband had founded. Now Thutmose was leaving as well. People were saying that a young prince called Tutankhaten would become Pharaoh and that under him Egypt would turn away from the Aten and changes that Akhenaten and Nefertiti had made.

A place of safety

IN ONE WALL OF THE STUDIO was an open cupboard fitted with stout wooden shelves. Thutmose decided that this would be a safe place to store the pieces of unfinished work and the beautiful portrait of Nefertiti. One by one he placed them carefully on a shelf. When they were all there, Thutmose took one final look round his studio before going to the door and letting himself out. He had already decided that the best way to protect the precious objects inside was to seal the entrance and plaster over the doorway. Perhaps he had a feeling that it would be a very long time before the studio would be opened again. By the time he had finished the work, the doorway blended in with the mud bricks of the studio walls. His treasures would be safe – Thutmose was confident about that when he climbed into his chariot and drove away from the city of Akhetaten.

Did he know that he would never return? That is something only the gods could foretell. Just three years after the coronation of the new young Pharaoh, Tutankhaten, the city of Akhetaten was deserted. Later stones used to construct the city's finest buildings were taken down to be used elsewhere. In time the rest of the buildings made of mud bricks disappeared beneath the sand and dust.

The young Pharaoh changed his name. Instead of Tutankhaten, he called himself Tutankhamun, which showed that he was a follower of the traditional Egyptian god, Amun, and not the Aten. In 1922 the world would be amazed by the treasures found buried with Tutankhamun in his tomb in the Valley of the Kings. But before that, in 1887, Thutmose's treasures were discovered when his studio was opened for the first time in three thousand five hundred years. Some of the pieces he had placed in the wall cupboard had broken when the shelves finally rotted away. However, the beautiful portrait of Nefertiti was preserved; only the piece of crystal was missing from her left eye.

Thutmose's wish had come true. After thousands of years people could once again look at his masterpiece and come face to face with Akhenaten's famous queen.

CHAPTER THREE

THE HARD PRICE OF BREAD

A story from 3200 years ago

Main characters in the story:

Nakht (*Nack-t*) – *a young weaver*
Mery (*Mer-ee*) – *a quarry worker*

INTRODUCTION

STONE WAS A VERY IMPORTANT MATERIAL to the ancient Egyptians. Stone was hard, and this hardness made it last for ever, or so people believed. That was why temples and tombs were built from stone. Most buildings in Egypt were built of mud bricks – even palaces were made in this way. People knew that mud brick buildings would one day crumble and disappear. But this would not happen with buildings made of stone. People believed that these would last into the afterlife, to be there for eternity.

But stone came at a price. It had to be hewn from quarries, and this was back-breaking work. Not many people would choose to do it. Men captured in wars used to be sent to the quarries. So were those who had been found guilty of committing a crime. That was why fourteen-year-old Nakht was down on his knees, banging at the hard granite with a heavy ball of dolerite rock. He had been caught stealing food, a piece of hard bread that had been dropped by a priest near the temple in Thebes where he worked.

It was hunger that had driven Nakht to eat the bread, even though he knew it was strictly forbidden. For the poor in ancient Egypt, being hungry was part of everyday life. It was something Nakht was used to.

PART ONE

A harsh punishment

YOU COULD HEAR THE NOISE FROM THE QUARRY a long way off. The sound of hundreds of heavy stone balls being pounded against the hard rock set up a drumming noise which spilled out from the hills across the plain to the banks of the River Nile. Nakht was almost deaf to the noise. He had been working in the quarry for four months, and the constant hammering had become another of the hardships he had to suffer – like the heat, the dust, the flies and the hunger. And it had been hunger that had sent Nakht to the quarry. That's what seemed so unfair to him.

Working in the quarry was a punishment. The work was difficult, but it had to be done; the huge granite blocks had to be cut from the hillside, so that they could be sent down the river to be used in the building of tombs or to be carved into statues of the gods or famous people.

Nakht never had very much to eat at the best of times, and finding the bread dropped by the priest had been too good a chance to miss. It was just bad luck that another priest had found him eating it in a shady corner of the temple precinct. Nakht had tried to explain that he had found the bread on the floor. But the priest refused to believe him. Nakht was only a lowly weaver in the temple. The priest thought he had stolen the bread from the temple bakery. So Nakht had lost his job in the temple and had been sent up the river to Aswan to work for six months in the granite quarries. He was fourteen years old and he was being punished like this over a piece of bread. The gods must really have had it in for him, he thought. How else could he have been so badly treated by them?

At the rock-face

THE EGYPTIANS USED DIFFERENT KINDS OF STONE to construct and decorate their sacred buildings like temples and tombs. One of the most popular of these was granite, the hard rock on which Nakht was now working. At first Egyptian builders found all the granite they needed in large loose boulders that lay around a valley close to Aswan, in the valley of the river Nile in the upper part of Egypt. As granite became more popular, the supply of loose boulders was used up. From then on this important stone had to be cut out of the ground, and once again the best place in Egypt to find granite was in the cliffs and sides of the valley near Aswan.

Egyptian workers did not have hard metal tools to cut rock. They used saws made of copper to cut limestone. But limestone is much softer than granite and even then the copper saws soon became blunt. The only way to cut through granite was to use tools made from a material that was harder than granite and the only suitable material was another rock called dolerite. So hundreds of workers like Nakht were given balls of dolerite rock with which to pound the granite and slowly break it up. The workers were organized into teams. Each worker had a section of rock on which he had to work, smashing his rock ball up and down, up and down, slowly, painfully slowly, chipping at the granite. By doing this, the team would begin to cut a trench about seventy-five centimetres wide all the way round the block of granite they wanted to remove. It took weeks of hammering to cut this trench, which had to be slightly deeper than the block of stone they wanted to remove. When the trench around the block was ready, the team would set to work cutting out enough rock beneath the block, so that it could be broken free with huge stone chisels or heavy wooden levers.

Stone and dust

MANY OF THE BLOCKS OF STONE CUT from the granite quarries at Aswan were used to make obelisks. Obelisks were tall stone pillars decorated with pictures and hieroglyphs before being set up as monuments or landmarks. These weighed hundreds of tons, though the biggest of all was still to be seen lying in the quarry. Whenever Nakht saw this huge obelisk he thought of the workmen who must have spent months and months on their knees patiently chipping at the rock around it. If it had ever been set up, this mighty obelisk would have stood over forty metres high and it would have weighed more than a thousand tons. Nakht felt sorry for the workmen who had toiled over this massive obelisk. After all their hard work it had never been moved from the quarry; in fact it had never been finally separated from the rock surrounding it. As the workers cut their trenches deeper around the obelisk, tiny cracks had started to appear. Work continued, but the cracks grew bigger until it became clear that the obelisk would split and break into pieces if they tried to detach it from the surrounding rock. Nakht could see where the quarrymen had tried to save part of the huge obelisk by re-cutting it, but this had not worked either, and in the end they had given up. What a waste of time and effort, he used to think to himself as he smashed his ball of dolerite up and down, up and down, hour after hour, day after day.

The work was boring, noisy and very uncomfortable. Nakht was used to squatting for hours in front of his weaver's loom in the temple workshop. That had been uncomfortable at first. But kneeling on the granite all the time had made his knees sore and stiff. They ached a lot now. The dust made Nakht cough a lot too. Sometimes he coughed so much that he felt as if his lungs were on fire. He was used to breathing in dust, you couldn't escape it in Egypt. But this granite dust in the quarries seemed to be sharper and more painful than the dust and sand of the desert.

Transporting the stone

ONCE A BLOCK OF GRANITE had been cut and levered free of the surrounding rock, it had to be transported to where it was needed. This involved more back-breaking work, because the heavy blocks had to be dragged over the ground. Some blocks were loaded onto wooden sledges, while others had heavy ropes tied to them, so that they could be pulled along. Either way, teams of men (and occasionally teams of oxen) pulled on the ropes to get the heavy blocks moving. When water was available, water-carriers moved in front of the blocks of stones, spreading water on the ground to make the surface slippery. This made the huge blocks easier to pull once they had started moving.

From the quarry, the stone blocks were dragged to the nearby bank of the River Nile. Here they were loaded onto special barges that were built to carry loads of up to five hundred tons. Once the stone was safely aboard, the barge was taken down the river to the site of the temple, tomb or other public place where it was going to be used. His work in the temple had shown Nakht how magnificent the blocks of red granite could look when they had been carved and polished and set in place. No wonder people thought that the gods approved of the hard everlasting stone. Working in the temple Nakht had admired the red granite, though he had never given a thought to where it came from, or to the hundreds of men who had toiled to hack it from the hillsides and drag it to and from the river to bring it to the temple. Little did he think that he would find himself doing that same work. Why should he? He was a teenager, and life as a weaver in the temple wasn't so bad. He had no way of knowing that one day he would join them, simply because he had eaten a piece of bread.

PART TWO

The weaver's trade

NAKHT'S FATHER HAD BEEN A WEAVER, so Nakht trained to be a weaver, too. That's what most boys in Egypt did at that time; they followed their father's trade. At one time weaving had been the work of women. Gradually men began to weave as well, though the material they wove was the same as the material that had been woven by women. This was called linen, and it was made from a plant called flax. Very little use was made of cotton or wool, and linen was the main cloth used in Egypt for thousands of years.

Like most jobs at that time, weaving linen was hard work. First the flax plants had to be spun into thread. The plants were harvested while they were still carrying their blue flowers, because young plants produced the best fibres. After harvesting, the stalks were cooked or dried in the sun. Then they were beaten and brushed with a comb called a hackle, to split each stalk into a mass of fibres.

These fibres were spun into thread which was set up on a loom. As the weaver wove the linen cloth, she (or he) would beat it tight with a bent stick. Over the centuries the cloth they wove became became finer and finer; eventually it was so fine that a length of linen could be pulled through a ring worn on someone's finger. Linen was used to make clothes for the living and to produce the lengths of thin cloth, like bandages, in which the bodies of important people were wrapped as part of the process of creating a mummy. The temple of Sethnakhte, where Nakht and his father worked, was like many temples in Egypt in having its own workshops where cloth and other goods were made. The flax used in the temple came from temple lands where it was grown and harvested by temple workers. In the workshop other workers spun the linen thread before weavers like Nakht wove the cloth which would be used to make clothes and sacred garments for the priests. Linen from the temple workshop was also sold to earn money for the temple.

The hours were long, but Nakht knew that working in the temple workshop was not as hard as other kinds of work in Egypt. For one thing he could work in the shade, away from the terrible heat that some workers had to suffer in the Egyptian summer. There was water to drink at the temple and, although he did not get paid very much, Nakht knew that as long as the temple existed, its workers would be paid their regular share of food and other goods.

Family life for the poor

OF COURSE, Nakht had to share what he earned with the other members of his family. He had brothers and sisters, as well as his father and mother, with whom he lived in their small, cramped house in a little village on the west bank of the Nile close to the temple. Their home was like every other building in the village. It was built of mud bricks. It had a flat roof, and it was crammed together with the other houses in a warren of narrow lanes. Inside the house there was one main room with small alcoves that formed bedrooms where the children slept. Nakht's parents slept in a cool cellar beneath the main room. The kitchen was an open-air room at the back of the house. The floor was made from beaten earth and the only windows were small holes in the wall, high up near the roof. Inside the house was shadowy and smoky because of the cooking fire at the back and the oil lamp that gave a feeble light.

The family had very little furniture. They did not have beds to sleep on or chairs to sit in. They ate their meals sitting on the floor, around a rush mat on which the food was served. And their food was simple. Like most Egyptians they ate a hard, rough bread and drank a kind of beer that was thick, almost as thick as a soup. Sometimes there was a little fish or meat to go with the meal. Sometimes there were a few dates or some beans, or perhaps some onions or leeks. The one thing Nakht could be sure of was that there was never enough to feed the whole family. That was why he felt hungry most of the time. Water had to be collected from the river in pottery jars, which Nakht's mother and older sisters did while he and his father were away during the day at work in the temple. The youngest children ran around naked, playing and getting in the way. Only the children of rich parents went to school.

Until he was sent up the river to the quarries at Aswan, Nakht had seen very little of Egypt outside his village. He used to watch the boats and barges passing up and down the river. In the markets on the bank he heard merchants and boatmen talking about distant cities on the Nile. For Nakht the whole world seemed to lie beside the great river. In his imagination that world was sandy, dusty and hot much of the time, and every year it was flooded as the great river rose over its banks and covered the land either side with a layer of rich, fertile black mud.

PART THREE

A hungry time of year

NAKHT HAD STARTED WORKING with his father when he was still a boy. Once he had learned the weaver's craft he was able to work at his own loom, squatting for hours in front of it, passing the thread from side to side between the rows of other thread and knocking the material tight every so often as the length of freshly woven linen grew in front of him. There were not many breaks and Nakht was stiff and aching when the time came to finish work and return home at the end of the day. Even when he was not working, Nakht felt uncomfortable much of the time. He had a lump on the sole of his foot which felt as if he was walking on a pebble the whole time. Nakht often had a pain in his tummy as well. Although he did not know it, he had parasites inside him which made him feel unwell. These made him feel even hungrier.

The day he found the piece of bread in the temple, Nakht had come to work without any food. It was a hungry time of the year before the new crops could be harvested, and food was in short supply. There had been no spare food in the house, so Nakht had gone to work knowing that he would not be able to eat anything until he returned home in the evening. It had been while he was taking a pile of new linen from the workshop to the temple store that Nakht had seen the bread lying in a corner where it had just fallen from a dish being carried by one of the priests. Nakht saw it and was tempted to stop and pick it up. But this was difficult because his arms were full with the folds of cloth. If the bread was still there when he returned in a few minutes, Nakht decided that he would take it.

And this is what he had done. He had quickly picked the lump of bread from the floor and hidden it in his hands. Then he had hurried to a shady corner of the temple precinct where he was eating it when the one of the priests who watched over the workers found him. The workshop was controlled very strictly. There were scribes who kept a record of every piece of material that was finished. There were also doorkeepers who kept a careful eye on everyone who came and went from the workshop. It had been the doorkeeper on duty who had noticed that Nakht was taking longer than he should have done to deliver the linen. He had told a passing priest and the priest had found Nakht guiltily eating the bread.

The justice of the gods

NAKHT MUST HAVE LOOKED SO SURPRISED and frightened that the priest immediately suspected that he had stolen it. Nakht was so scared that he didn't know what to say, and when he did try to speak his words came out in a jumble which only made him look more guilty. Nakht was short, even for a poor fourteen-year-old Egyptian weaver. The priest had seized his arm and had dragged him back to the workshop. The senior scribe was in charge of the workshop, and when the priest told him that he suspected Nakht of stealing bread from the temple bakery, the scribe laid down his writing brush and looked sternly at Nakht.

The teenage boy in front of him looked terrified, and the priest knew that he could lose his right to work in the temple for ever. Stealing food in the temple was like stealing food from the spirit of Sethnakhte, who needed it in the afterlife. However, the senior scribe was a kind man. And when Nakht sobbed that he been eating the bread because he was so hungry and because there so little food at home, the priest decided to be lenient.

'What you have done displeases the gods,' he told Nakht. 'But the gods are just and lenient. They understand that you are young. So they allow you to make good your crime, and when you have shown them that you are truly sorry, you may return here to the temple of Sethnakhte, and you may continue your work as a weaver.'

Nakht was confused. 'What is it that I must do? How can I show the gods these things?'

'By working to bring the precious stone with which we show glory to the gods,' said the chief scribe. 'You will be sent to the quarries at Aswan where the red granite is found. For half a year you will work there to show the gods your repentance. After that you may return and we will consider the matter closed.'

'And my father?' asked Nakht, who was terrified that his father might be punished as well.

'As I tell you, the gods are just and lenient,' said the chief scribe. 'He had no part in this. So he will not suffer for what you, his son, have done.'

Nakht felt relieved to hear this. He was scared at the idea of being sent away from home, but at least his family would come to no harm. His mother cried when she heard what had happened. She cried because her son had got into trouble and was now being sent away. But she also cried because it had been his hunger that had caused his trouble – and she knew that there was nothing she could do to make things easier for him.

PART FOUR

Life in the quarries

SO NAKHT HAD LEFT HOME on one of the barges sailing up the river to collect stone from the Aswan quarries. If he had not been frightened about what might happen to him in the quarries, the voyage up the river would have been an exciting adventure. All that Nakht could think about, however, was the voyage down river in a half a year's time, when his punishment would be over.

Work in the quarries was hard, but life in the quarry town was not that different to life at home. Nakht shared a mud brick house with the family of a man in charge of a team that spilt the blocks of granite from the bedrock. His name was Mery, and because his work was skilled he was better paid than most quarry workers; Nakht joined his family like another son.

Soon it became difficult to distinguish one day from another. Life for Nakht fell into a dull routine of dust and hammering and heat, of aching knees and sore fingers. At night he lay curled up on the floor in a corner of the house, feeling hungry inside. As the weeks passed he noticed that his cough grew worse because of the sharp granite dust. After four months had passed Nakht was looking ill, and Mery decided he should speak to one of the officials who oversaw the quarry.

'The boy cannot work properly,' Mery explained. 'His health is weak. Has he not paid his penance? Are not the gods satisfied by what he has done?'

The official asked to see Nakht and when he was brought to him, he asked Nakht to tell him why he had been sent to the quarries.

'I was eating bread in the temple precinct,' Nakht told him.

'And who did the bread belong to?' asked the official.

'It belonged to the gods, because it was in the temple?'

'If you find any bread in the temple ever again, will you eat that too?'

'No – never… never again… ' Nakht promised and his voice gave way to painful coughing.

'Then I think you should return to your work in the temple, to show Sethnakhte and the gods that you mean this.'

'You mean I can go home?' gasped Nakht between coughs.

'Yes, go home,' said the official. 'And remember what you have learned – that the gods are just and lenient.'

An early release

THERE WAS A BARGE LEAVING with a load of stone the following day. Nakht had very few belongings to take with him, so it took no time to pack up and be ready to go. He thanked Mery and his family for their kindness and asked them to meet his family if they ever came to his village. What a surprise his parents and his brothers and sisters would have when he arrived home nearly two months earlier than expected.

This time Nakht could look forward to his journey down the great river. He waved goodbye to his friends as the barge pulled away and began to move downstream with the flow of the water. When they were out of sight, he found somewhere to sit at the front of the big boat where he could enjoy the sights they passed. Slowly the hills and cliffs of Aswan were left behind, though the drumming noise took longer to fade from his ears. You could hear the noise from the quarry a long way off. That was a sound Nakht would never forget.

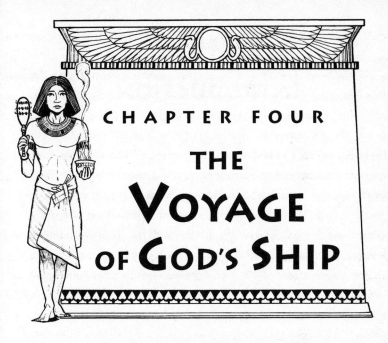

CHAPTER FOUR

THE

VOYAGE

OF GOD'S SHIP

A story from 3070 years ago

Main characters in the story:

Wenamun (*When-a-mun*) – *a priest in the Temple of Karnak*

Herihor (*Heh-ree-haw*) – *high priest in the Temple of Karnak*

Mengebet (*Men-ge-bet*) – *a ship's captain*

Nesbanebded (*Nez-bah-neb-dead*) – *ruler of Lower Egypt*

Tentamun (*Ten-tar-mun*) – *wife of Nesbanebded*

Beder (*Beh-derr*) – *ruler of the city of Dor*

Tjikarba'al (*Chick-ah-barl*) – *prince of Byblos*

Hatiba (*Hah-tee-bar*) – *ruler of Alasiya*

Tentne (*Tent-neh*) – *a singer*

Introduction

ONCE, EGYPT HAD been a force to reckon with, the mightiest power of the surrounding territories. Egypt controlled all the nations round about. But by Wenamun's time, Egypt's power was fading. Where once rulers of surrounding countries would have obeyed the Pharaoh and his representatives without question, now they felt free not simply to disobey, but to be openly hostile. It was against this background that Wemamun, a priest of the Temple of Karnak, was sent on a once-in-a-lifetime adventure to distant lands.

PART ONE

Boats and ships

BOATS AND SHIPS – Wenamun had always been fascinated by boats and ships. Right from the time when he was still very young, boats and ships slipped through his memory just as he had seen them moving up and down the broad River Nile. Even though he was now grown up and serving as a priest in the great temple at Karnak, dedicated to the god Amun, Wenamun had never lost his interest in boats and ships. If anything it had grown stronger.

Most Egyptians grew up living close to the Nile. The river brought life itself to the dry desert lands. It brought water to drink and water that made the crops grow. Every year the Nile flooded over its banks, leaving rich black mud in which farmers could plant their crops when the waters retreated at the start of the growing season. But the Nile was also the main 'highway' of the kingdom. For hundreds of miles it flowed slowly northwards through Egypt towards the open sea, and up and down it the people of Egypt had paddled and sailed boats of all sizes for thousands of years, almost as long as people had been living beside the river.

Wenamun could still remember the smell and feel of the first boat he had been in. It was like small boats used everywhere in Egypt for fishing or travelling short distances. This boat had been made from papyrus reeds which grew beside the river. Bundles of reeds had been tied together to make a long tube shape which curved up out of the water at both ends. Sitting in the bottom of the boat for the first time, Wenamun had been just big enough to look over the edge across the smooth water of the river. Behind him sat his father who paddled the reed boat at the back. In front of Wenamun was his uncle, who paddled the boat at the other end. Sometimes other members of the family came as well. At other times, when he was older, Wenamun travelled alone with his father, carrying goods to market in the village further down the river. Reed boats like this were easy to make and as Wenamun's family grew, their boats got bigger too.

However, reed boats could not carry heavy loads, like the

stone which had to be taken by river from quarries to temples and other important buildings that were being constructed. For journeys like this wooden boats were needed, and Wenamun still felt a thrill of excitement whenever he saw one of these long, graceful craft come into view.

Although boats made of wood were longer and wider than reed boats, they had the same distinctive shape: a flat bottom which ran into upturned points at both ends. This meant that most of the boat was above the water so that it could pass over places where the water in the river was shallow. In fact many wooden boats could be taken apart and carried past obstacles further up the river.

All but a few wooden boats in Egypt were made from short planks of wood held together with wooden pegs and ropes that lashed the boards tightly together. Most boats on the Nile used oars, though some were towed by a rope from the bank and others were fitted with a large square sail. Steering was hard work for the helmsman at the back, who had to use all his strength to push and pull one, and sometimes two, big steering oars.

The most expensive boats, the ones owned by the temples, the Pharaoh and the other rich people in the kingdom, were made of long planks of wood. These were more expensive because the tree trunks from which long planks were cut had to be brought to Egypt from other countries. Cedar wood was highly prized. It came from the mountain forests which lay to the east. Only the finest ships were made of this expensive wood, and they were magnificent. The Pharaoh's pleasure barge had a royal cabin covered with gold, the hull was painted in bright colours and the sail was made of finely woven material. This was the most magnificent boat Wenamun had ever seen.

A very special boat

WENAMUN'S DUTIES IN THE TEMPLE meant that he was responsible for a boat every bit as important as these expensive vessels. This boat did not belong to the Pharaoh, however – it belonged to the great god Amun.

Boats were an important part of the religious life in Egypt, just as they were an important part of daily life. People believed that the souls of the dead joined the sun on its journey through the Upper Waters, another name for the heavens that surrounded the world. This was why model boats and sometimes complete, full-sized boats were placed in tombs as part of a burial. Special funeral boats carried the bodies of the dead to the burial sites on the west bank of the River Nile. And because humans made so much use of boats in life and death, it was only right that Amun should have a special boat as well.

The god's boat was known as a solar boat. Every New Year a statue of Amun was placed in this beautifully built and magnificently decorated boat, which was then carried by a team of priests from the Temple of Karnak to the Temple of Luxor. Even when the solar boat was stored back inside the temple, people believed that Amun still sailed the skies every day in the form of the sun carried in two ships – one ship for the morning, one for the afternoon. At the end of the day, as evening approached, Amun arrived in the west, the land of the dead. Here he brought light and warmth before sailing on into the night, until he reappeared at dawn the next day.

The solar boat of the god Amun was the most important of all the boats and ships that belonged to the temple. Keeping the boat looking smart and shipshape was an important way of showing honour and respect to the god. So when the boat needed repairs or replacing, no time and no expense could be spared in making it fit for the god. And this was the situation that now faced Wenamun.

For him it was a privilege and a pleasure to look after the god's ship, but it was also a great responsibility. When the solar boat had last been carried from the temple, he had noticed worrying signs. Some of the wood was weak. In places the boards were coming apart. Paint was cracking. But the god's ship needed more than a coat of paint; many parts of it needed rebuilding, and for this new wood would have to be used. In fact, when Wenamun looked closely at the solar boat it became clear that Amun might need a completely new one.

For the honour of Amun

A SPECIAL MEETING OF THE TEMPLE PRIESTS was called so that Wenamun could tell them the serious news. They all understood what had to be done, even though the cost of buying all the expensive new wood, not to mention the cost of sailing to distant lands to fetch it and bring it home, would be very high. Egypt was no longer richer and more powerful than its neighbouring countries. The voyage would be more difficult than similar voyages in the past, but if Amun was not honoured with a shiny, sturdy solar boat, the priests feared that Egypt might grow weaker still.

So it was arranged that Wenamun would undertake this important voyage from Karnak all the way down the river to the sea, and then around the coast to Byblos, where the wood could be bought. From the temple treasury he was given one gold vessel, four silver jugs and a purse containing more silver – enough precious metal to pay for the cost of the voyage and all the wood needed for the solar barge.

PART TWO

Setting sail

WHEN ALL THE PREPARATIONS WERE MADE, Wenamun said his last prayers in the temple before the voyage, asking Amun to protect them and bring them safely back to Karnak with their precious cargo of wood. Then he said farewell to the other priests and went aboard the large sea-going ship on which he would journey to Byblos. Temple servants came with him, and so did a statue of Amun, which was housed in a special place in the ship to show that the god himself was sailing with them. As the priests on the banks chanted prayers, the ropes were cast off and the crew started to row the god's ship down the river. Some of the smaller temple boats kept them company for a while, but one by one they turned round and headed for home, leaving Wenamun and his companions to their voyage.

The crew did not need to use the oars all the time. When the wind was blowing from behind, they were able to hoist the large square sail and let the breeze carry them down the river. At night they moored by the bank, where they set up camp or found shelter in one of the villages or small towns that lined the river. However, their first important port of call was Tanis, a town which lay in the Nile delta, not far from the sea. Here Wenamun went ashore to pay his respects to Nesbanebded. Nesbanebded reigned over Lower Egypt for the Pharaoh, Rameses XI, who seems no longer to have had any real control over Egypt.

Nesbanebded and his wife, Tentamun, received Wenamun in the hall where all important visitors were greeted. Wenamun presented them with letters of introduction from Herihor, high priest of the Temple of Amun. These gave the orders for his voyage, which had come from Amun. They were read aloud, and when Nesbanebded had heard them he announced solemnly, 'We will do as Amun-Re, King of the Gods, our lord, has said.' These were the words Wenamun had been hoping to hear, for with them Nesbanebded had given Wenamun his official permission to sail from Egypt to Byblos, to complete his mission.

After their long voyage down the river, the crew needed to

restock the ship with fresh food and water and to take on other stores for the sea part of their voyage. So Wenamun stayed with Nesbanebded and Tentamun for several days until everything was ready.

As soon as Mengebet, captain of the ship, was satisfied that they had everything needed for the voyage, he sent word to Wenamun. Nesbanebded and Tentamun came to see the travellers off, and stayed watching from the river bank until Wenamun's ship had disappeared round a bend in the wide river delta. Before long Wenamun began to sense a different movement in the ship. In place of the smooth passage through the waters of the Nile, there was a gentle lifting and falling which became a steady rhythm as the river banks faded further and further from view. The ship had left Egypt behind. The movement Wenamun could feel was the easy swell of what Mengebet and other sailors called 'the great sea of Syria'. The main part of Wenamun's adventure was under way at last.

Disaster strikes

EGYPTIAN SHIPS WERE NOT AS WELL DESIGNED FOR SEA TRAVEL as the ships used in other countries around 'the great sea of Syria'. Finding your way at sea could be difficult as well, which is why most sailors liked to stay in sight of land if they could. This is what Mengebet did, and once the ship had left the delta of the River Nile he used the two big steering oars to point the ship to the north-east. The sailors hauled on the ropes and secured the sail, while Wenamun found somewhere to sit in the shade where he could enjoy the sound of water running under the hull as the ship cut through the clear blue water.

The first port they called at was the city of Dor, where the ruler, a prince named Beder, greeted Wenamun politely and commanded food to be sent to the ship. Before long Beder's servants arrived with fifty loaves of newly baked bread, a large flagon of wine and fresh meat. That night Wenamun, Mengebet and the sailors enjoyed a feast that none of them would ever forget. Unfortunately for Wenamun it was not only the delicious food and wine that would remind him of his visit to Dor. Some time during the night disaster struck, and when he woke in the morning he discovered that something unspeakably dreadful had happened. While he had been asleep, all the gold and silver that Wenamun was taking to Byblos to buy the wood for Amun's ship had disappeared.

'Wake up! Wake up!' Wenamun shouted, shaking Menegebet roughly where he lay asleep on the deck.

'What's the matter?' asked the captain crossly. His head was aching and he had been looking forward to a good long sleep after the feast the night before.

'Search the ship,' Wenamun ordered. 'Look everywhere. It must be found. . . it must be found.'

'What must be found?' asked Mengebet, sitting up stiffly and rubbing his eyes.

'All the gold. All the silver. All the coins I was given from the Temple of Amun. They've disappeared and I don't know what has happened to them.'

Mengebet was lost for words. Like many sailors, he was very worried by any bad luck that happened on a voyage. Losing treasure belonging to the great god Amun was about as bad as bad luck could get. His sleepiness disappeared like a dream. Mengebet jumped to his feet and moved around the ship, kicking the sailors awake and yelling to them to begin searching the ship.

Their search did not last long. Sadly for Wenamun they did not find the god's treasure, but they did discover what had happened to it. As Mengebet and his men began pulling aside their stores and looking through hatches to see if the treasure was under the deck, they realized that one of the sailors was missing. He had been on the ship the night before, though he had stayed in the shadows and hadn't joined in the singing and dancing with his shipmates. Now, in the morning, the sailor had vanished and so had Amun's treasure.

Search for a thief

THERE WAS NO TIME TO LOSE. Although it was still early in the morning, Wenamun hurried to the palace of Prince Beder in the heart of the city, and banged and banged his fists on the heavy wooden gates until they were opened and he could rush inside.

The prince was still in his bedchamber when Wenamun was shown in to him. 'I have been robbed in your harbour. . . You must search for my money,' cried Wenamun, who then explained what had happened.

The prince listened until Wenamun had finished speaking. But the way he treated his visitor was not the same as it had been when Wenamun had first arrived in the harbour of Dor. Instead of showing that he was concerned, Beder shrugged his shoulders and asked, 'Are you sure about what has happened? Because it sounds as though it was one of your own men who robbed you, not one of mine. If one of my people had gone down to your ship and stolen your money, I would have replaced your treasure myself until we could find the thief; but from what you say, it was one of your crew who did this. Why not stay here for a few days while we search for him?'

Despite his words, there was something about the way Beder spoke which made Wenamun suspect that the prince would not be searching very thoroughly for the thief. And his suspicions proved to be right. Day after day Wenamun waited for news from the palace. The hot hours of daylight passed. He paced up and down the quay, watching other ships hoisting their sails and heading out to sea. How he wanted to join them – to find Amun's treasure, cast off the mooring ropes and continue his voyage to Byblos.

But there was no word from Prince Beder, and no sign of the thief. Each night when he settled down under the stars to sleep, Wenamun tried to imagine where the sailor with the stolen treasure might be. How far could he travel in a day? In which direction had he gone? Not back to Egypt, that would be too dangerous. With so much treasure, though, the sailor could afford to buy his escape on a ship sailing to any port across 'the great sea of Syria'. The one thing that Wenamun could be certain of was this: as each day passed the thief could be further and further from Dor, further and further from being caught.

After nine days of waiting, Wenamun had had enough. Angrily he stormed into the palace, demanding to see the prince. 'Look, you have not found my money,' he told him. Beder, however, did not seem very worried. How different this would have been in the past, thought Wenamun to himself. When Egypt was rich and powerful, no one, not even a prince of Dor, would have dared treat a priest of Amun in the way he was being treated.

Beder would not help him, Wenamun could see that. So he returned to his ship and ordered Mengebet to set sail without the treasure. After nine wasted days, Wenamun again felt the movement of the sea and the wind carrying his ship along the coast, but now his voyage was filled with worry and fear. Would Amun be angry? Would the god punish Wenamun for what had happened? What would happen to him if he returned to Karnak without the wood for the god's solar boat? Boats and ships – Wenamun's love of boats and ships had turned to fear.

PART THREE

With the help of Amun

AFTER LEAVING DOR, Wenamun's ship stopped for a short time in the port of Tyre and then sailed on to Byblos, where

Tjikarba'al was the prince. In the harbour at Byblos Wenamun discovered a ship carrying almost as much silver as had been stolen from him. There was no time to waste and, acting like a powerful Egyptian commander of days gone by, Wenamun ordered his men to seize the ship. His plan was to hold it as a ransom until the treasure of Amun was returned.

However, Tjikarba'al did not show Wenamun the respect that he might have done in the days when Egypt's power controlled all the nations round about. Instead of offering to help catch the thief, he sent an order to Wenamun, telling him 'Get away from my harbour.'

By this time Wenamun had brought the statue of Amun ashore to hide it in a place where he could be sure it would be safe. When he received Tjikarba'al's order, he replied, 'Where shall I go? If you can find me a ship, I'll go back to Egypt.'

Yet Tjikarba'al refused to help. Each day he sent a messenger with the same order: 'Get away from my harbour.' And so it continued for twenty-nine days, until a miracle happened.

Tjikarba'al was in the temple making an offering to his god when a young man serving as a temple attendant suddenly fell into a frenzy, and began calling out so that everyone in the temple could hear his voice: 'Bring me the god and his messenger, for he has been sent by Amun himself.'

That same night, Wenamun had finally found a ship on which he could sail home to Egypt. What choice did he have? His situation looked hopeless. All his treasure had been stolen. He had no money to buy wood for the solar boat of Amun.

Unless he sailed on this ship to Egypt, he might have to wait months before he reached home. With a heavy heart Wenamun had loaded his possessions onto the ship. Now he was waiting for night to fall before he carried aboard the statue of Amun, so that no other eyes should see the god.

Suddenly there was a sound of hurrying feet. Fearing the worst, Wenamun moved away from where the statue of Amun lay hidden. The sound of the feet grew closer, and then a small crowd of men ran out from between the buildings and onto the quay. They looked around until one of them spotted Wenamun, and they all raced towards him. Wenamun made ready to defend himself, but the men did not attack him. The harbour master, whom Wenamun had come to know during the past weeks, had brought a new message from Tjikarba'al. Only this time the prince was ordering Wenamun to stay! 'The prince says to wait here till tomorrow,' the harbour master told him.

Poor Wenamun could hardly believe his ears. After being told every day for nearly a month to leave the harbour, he was suddenly being commanded to stay. It didn't make sense. The harbour master sent a messenger to check with the prince that he really did want Wenamun to stay and the answer came back, 'Stay'. Wearily Wenamun unloaded his possessions and settled down for another night by the harbour at Byblos.

What was going to happen to him tomorrow? What could possibly have happened to make Tjikarba'al change his mind? Wenamun didn't know. All he had was his hope, and his faith in Amun.

The fury of a priest

THE FOLLOWING MORNING Tjikarba'al summoned Wenamun to him. The two men met in the upper chamber of the palace, which looked out over the sea. Tjikarba'al asked Wenamun how long it was since he had left home.

'Five whole months', was his heartfelt reply.

The prince then asked for the letters Wenamun had been given by Herihor, high priest of the Temple of Amun, which introduced him and explained the purpose of his voyage. These had been left with Nesbanebded and Tentamun, he told the prince. But this only made Tjikarba'al angry. Wisely Wenamun kept his silence until the prince quietened down and finally asked, 'On what commission have you come?'

This gave Wenamun the chance to impress the prince with the power and authority that he had been given for the voyage. Standing before Tjikarba'al, Wenamun told him solemnly, 'I have come in search of wood for the ship of Amun-Re, king of the gods. Your father and your grandfather gave wood for this. I order you to do the same!'

If Wenamun had hoped to overawe the prince with this command, he was disappointed. 'So they did,' agreed Tjikarba'al. 'My people provided materials, but only after Pharaoh had sent six ships filled with fine Egyptian goods for our storehouses. But you – what have you brought us?'

Of course, Wenamun had no answer to this. To make things worse, Tjikarba'al commanded the old records to be brought to him, and in them he showed Wenamun the list of all the great riches that his father and his grandfather had been paid when they had supplied wood for the solar boat of Amun. If Egypt had paid so much before, Tjikarba'al asked, why should he not be paid the same for supplying the same amount of wood?

Some men might have admitted defeat at this point. Wenamun's case looked hopeless. But Herihor and the other priests had chosen wisely when they sent Wenamun to fetch the timber from Byblos. Having come this far and having been made to wait so long, first in Dor then in Byblos itself, he was not going to go home without one final effort.

Tjikarba'al had insulted him by calling his voyage 'a pointless journey you have been forced to make.' In reply Wenamun answered angrily, 'Nonsense! This journey is not pointless! I am here on a mission to serve Amun-Re. Amun is the king of the gods, and you own nothing which doesn't already belong to him – the woods, the seas, every boat on the river is Amun's. Amun is all-powerful, and I am here on his business!'

Tjikarba'al had not expected Wenamun to answer him so strongly. He was taken aback and this let Wenamun continue his attack by blaming Tjikarba'al for keeping Amun waiting: 'And now, you have let this great god spend twenty-nine days moored in your harbour without your knowing!'

Like a boxer who has stunned his opponent with a sudden burst of unexpected punches, Wenamun had overcome Tjikarba'al. While the prince was still reeling from what he had been told, Wenamun called for a scribe and quickly wrote a letter to Nesbanebded and Tentamun in Tanis, asking them to send the rich gifts Tjikarba'al was asking for.

This turnaround had happened so quickly that Tjikarba'al still seemed in a daze when Wenamun's letter was given to a royal messenger, with orders to sail immediately to Tanis to deliver it to Nesbanebded and Tentamun in person. Better still, some of the wood for Amun's solar boat was also loaded onto the messenger's ship. This wood happened to be in the harbour at Byblos, and Wenamun didn't waste any time in having it put aboard the ship bound for Tanis and the Nile.

Amun hears his servant

AS THE SHIP SAILED AWAY FROM BYBLOS, Wenamun had reason to feel very pleased. His quick thinking and stern talking had turned the tables on Tjikarba'al. And now there was a chance that he would be able to return to Egypt with the timber after all. Perhaps the god was rewarding him for his determination. He would not be disappointed.

When the messenger's ship returned from Tanis, it was laden with the goods that Nesbanebded and Tentamun had sent in payment for the wood for the solar boat. There were objects made of gold and silver, fine linen, five hundred ox hides, five hundred mats, five hundred ropes, twenty sacks of lentils and thirty baskets of fish. When Tjikarba'al saw all these being unloaded he was overjoyed, and immediately sent three hundred men and three hundred oxen to the forests to cut down and fetch the trees that Wenamun had travelled so far and so long to find.

The trees were felled that winter – as many as Wenamun had asked for, and of the best quality. They would make fine straight boards for the god's solar boat. When summer came again, the heavy logs were dragged from the forest and brought to the shore of 'the great sea of Syria' where they would be loaded onto the ships taking them to Egypt. Tjikarba'al summoned Wenamun once again and told him that the timber was ready to be taken to Egypt. In reply Wenamun told the prince that Amun would reward him for his service by giving Tjikarba'al a long and happy life. Then they parted, and Wenamun began what he hoped would be the final part of his long voyage. All he had to do now was to load the tree trunks aboard his ships and set sail for Egypt and home.

PART FOUR

A sting in the tail

HOWEVER, THERE WAS ONE FINAL STING in the tail of the story of Amun's faithful servant. Standing on the shore, watching the tree trunks being loaded, Wenamun caught sight of a group of ships sailing towards him. He counted eleven sails, and as the ships grew closer a terrible fear came over him – they were Tjekker ships, from the city of Dor, where Wenamun's troubles had begun. As soon as they saw him, the Tjekker sailors shouted out, 'Take him prisoner! Don't let him get away to Egypt!'

At that moment it must have seemed to Wenamun that the great god Amun had finally deserted him. Things would never have been like this in the old days, he thought bitterly to himself. When Egypt was rich and powerful, no one would have dared treat Amun's loyal servant in this way. How times had changed. The more he thought about it, the sadder he felt, and in the end Wenamun sat down on the sand alone and wept tears of anger and helplessness.

It was the prince's scribe who found him and tried to comfort him. Wenamun told him what had happened 'And see, they've come to take me prisoner again,' he wept.

The scribe knew who the men aboard the Tjekker ships were. He knew they were enemies of old who could see their chance to bring harm to Egypt. So he went quickly to the prince to tell him about Wenamun. The story Tjikarba'al heard was so sad and so hopeless that, in spite of disagreements he had had in the past with Wenamun, he also began to weep with pity for Amun's servant, who had been stopped yet again from returning home. But Tjikarba'al did more than weep. He commanded his scribe to go back to Wenamun, to give him two flagons of wine and a sheep to roast. He also sent an Egyptian singing-woman called Tentne to raise the poor man's spirits. 'Sing to him, and tell him not to worry,' the prince told Tentne.

Tjikarba'al's scribe gave Wenamun a similar message from the prince, 'Eat and drink, and don't worry. I'll have news for you tomorrow.'

So Wenamun settled down for another night by the harbour

at Byblos, although for the first time in a month he had something tasty to eat, good wine to drink and songs to remind him of home.

In the hands of Amun

THE NEXT MORNING Tjikarba'al summoned his council and the men from the Tjekker ships, and Wenamun as well. They all met in the prince's council chamber, where Tjikarba'al demanded to know why the Tjekker had ordered Wenamun to be captured and held prisoner.

Their answer was simple. The Tjekker people had long been in conflict with Egypt, they explained. Wenamun was an important Egyptian, so wasn't it obvious that they would want to capture him? After all, a priest from the great Temple of Amun would make a very valuable hostage.

Wenamun tried not to show his fear, for frightened he was. He waited for Tjikarba'al's reply. 'I can't imprison the servant of Amun,' the prince told the Tjekker sailors. But then he added words that would have made many men turn pale with terror. 'Let me send him away, and then you can hunt him down and capture him.' Perhaps Tjikarba'al had changed his mind about helping Wemanum, or perhaps he thought his decision was fair. Either way, Wenamum was in trouble.

So that was it, Wenamun realised. It was going to be a hunt – a game of cat and mouse. Tjikarba'al would let him make for the open sea in his ships, then the Tjekker ships would sail after them and try to capture the ships, the wood for Amun's solar boat, the statue of Amun and Wenamun himself. His fate, he knew, lay in the wind, and the power of the wind rested with Amun alone.

So the two fleets made ready in the harbour at Byblos. Sailors checked their sails and their ropes. The heavy tree trunks were tied down securely. To keep down weight on the ships Wenamun took only the water they needed for a short voyage. One way or the other, he thought, this voyage of escape would not last long. Either he would get away from the Tjekker ships and reach a friendly port, or he would be captured and taken back to Dor. Alone with the statue of Amun, Wenamun prayed to the god for a safe return home. Then he gave the order to hoist the sails and placed his fate in the hands of his god.

Amun's answer

AMUN WAS NOT DEAF. He heard his faithful servant's prayer for help. As the sun moved across the midday sky Amun sent a wind that carried Wenamun's ships swiftly over the waves away from Byblos towards the west. As the sun god travelled through the afternoon sky, he carried Wenamun and his ships with him. Far behind, the Tjekker sailors watched Wenamun's fleet disappear over the horizon and out of sight.

And so Wenamun's voyage began its final chapter. Amun did not carry him home right away. The wind sent from the god blew Wenamun's ships to the island of Alasiya, which is called Cyprus today. There he was attacked by hostile natives who might have killed him had he not been able to reach Hatiba, the queen of the region. Through an interpreter Wenamun warned her that if any harm came to the sailors from Byblos, Tjikarba'al would sail to Alasiya to take revenge. As he said this, Wenamun must have thought back to a time when the threat of revenge from Egypt itself would have made a local ruler obey his command. But those days had gone and now it was Tjikarba'al's name and the threat of attack from Byblos that made rulers like Hatiba take notice.

In time Wenamun did return to Egypt and the safety of sailing home to Karnak up the River Nile. The solar boat was made ready for Amun and the god smiled down from the heavens on Wenamun, the faithful priest who had faced the dangers and discomforts of a long voyage to bring the precious wood for the most important boat in the temple.

Boats and ships – Wenamun had always been fascinated by boats and ships, but after the voyage of god's ship, he would think twice before he next sailed too far from home.

CHAPTER FIVE

THE **MAGIC**
OF THE **LAST**
EGYPTIAN
PHARAOH

A story from 2350 years ago

Main characters in the story:

Nectanebo II (*Nect-a-neebo*) – *the last Egyptian Pharaoh of Egypt*

Teos (*Tay-oss*) – *son of Nectanebo I*

Horus (*Hore-us*) – *the falcon-headed god beloved of Nectanebo*

Osiris (*O-sire-us*) – *a god, father of Horus*

Isis (*Eye-sis*) – *wife of Osiris*

Seth – *brother of Osiris*

INTRODUCTION

IN 343BC, EGYPT was a stable, independent kingdom. It was free from the rule of the Persian empire, which had conquered Egypt two centuries earlier. However, the Egyptian army was smaller and less powerful than in the days of Egypt's glory, when Pharaohs had been able to command men to leave their fields and farms and fight for their ruler. Many of the soldiers now were from other countries, and had to be paid for their services. Egypt was vulnerable to attack from its enemies, and one day came the attack that Pharaoh Nactenebo II, himself a former warrior, had hoped would not happen. He was going to have to use every weapon at his disposal to defeat the invading army – including magic.

PART ONE

Enemies in Egypt

THE HOT SUMMER SUN BEAT DOWN on the palace courtyard. A small crowd of courtiers and servants had gathered round the chariot that minutes earlier had rattled through the gateway kicking up a plume of dust stretching behind, back in the direction of the frontier. The driver of the chariot had been hot, sticky and very thirsty after hours of travelling along bumpy roads. But even before his horses had pulled to a complete halt, he had jumped down and run to the palace doorway, shouting to the guards that he had an urgent message for the Pharaoh, Nectanebo. The Pharaoh's chamberlain had met the messenger and listened to what he had to say. Then he had slowly turned and made his way back to the inner part of the palace, where the Pharaoh was finishing prayers in his private temple dedicated to the god Horus. Bowing low, the chamberlain announced solemnly, 'There is a message, your Highness.'

The tone in his voice told Nectanebo that the message brought bad news. 'Does it come from the frontier?'

'It comes from Pelusium, oh mighty one. The city has fallen to the enemy. The Persians are coming.'

The Pharaoh answered with a nod of his head and then told his chamberlain, 'Leave me, please. Send word to the generals defending the city that I will meet them at noon in the council chamber. Tell the chief priests of the temples to be there as well. Now go. I will call for you shortly.'

The chamberlain bowed again and left the royal temple of Horus, closing the doors behind him with a heavy thud.

A Pharaoh and a god

NECTANEBO STOOD IN FRONT OF THE STATUE of the god, gazing in silence at its head, shaped like a falcon.

Throughout their long history the kings of Egypt had been closely linked with Horus. Egyptian religion taught that Horus was the son of Osiris, the god of farming, death and rebirth, who had once ruled Egypt as a Pharaoh. But legends told how Osiris had been murdered by his jealous brother Seth. He had cut up Osiris's body and hidden the pieces. However, Osiris's wife, Isis, had found the pieces and miraculously put them back together again. She had given birth to Horus, who had defeated Seth and driven him out of the kingdom for ever. After this Horus became the new Pharaoh. Osiris became king of the dead and Isis became the goddess of magic and life.

For Nectanebo, though, the connection with Horus reached beyond royal tradition. Horus had fought his enemy, Seth. He had beaten him and had forced him to flee. By doing this Horus had protected his kingdom, Egypt. For all of his sixteen years as Pharaoh, this is what Nectanebo had been doing as well. Whenever Egyptians looked at statues and carvings of Horus, Nectanebo wanted them to think of him. He wanted his people to believe that he was Nectanebo the Falcon – the king who saved and protected his people and the kingdom from their enemies.

Troubled times

NECTANEBO HAD BECOME KING at a troubled time in the history of Egypt. Two centuries earlier the Persians had conquered the country. Egypt had lost its independence and for the next one hundred and twenty-one years it had been governed as a province of the vast Persian empire. These had been dark days for the Egyptian people. Even when the country had become independent again, the people no longer felt as confident and easy as they once had.

That had been forty-five years before Nectanebo had become Pharaoh. Although Egypt was free once more, it no longer had powerful armies and a strong government. More and more soldiers and officials came from other countries and settled in Egypt. Many of them came from the city-states of Greece. They expected to be paid for their help and they expected payment in money. Egypt did not have much metal to make money, so most of the coins paid to foreign soldiers and government officials had to be bought from other countries. A lot of this foreign money was paid for by the temples in Egypt, which had grown rich down the centuries.

The last Egyptian Pharaoh

THE KING STANDING BEFORE THE STATUE of Horus on that hot summer morning in 343BC was not the first Egyptian Pharaoh to be called Nectanebo. He was actually the second. Nectanebo I had been his uncle. He had defended Egypt against more attacks from Persia. He had made the frontiers strong and under his rule Egypt had been safe. Nectanebo I had fought the Persians when they had tried to invade Egypt, but he had stopped short of sending his armies into Persian territory. That would have been too risky.

However, when Nectanebo I had been succeeded by his son, Teos, the prince had decided to ignore his father's example. Instead of concentrating on making the frontiers strong against the enemy, Teos had sent his army to attack Persian bases on the coast of the great sea of Syria. This had been a disaster. There had been strong rivalry between the commanders of the new Pharaoh's army who came from Egypt and those who came from Greece. After several battles with the Persians, the Egyptian army began to fall apart and many of the soldiers had deserted Teos. They left him and joined the army that was gathering around his nephew. He was an Egyptian general whom the soldiers trusted. When his uncle fled Egypt and escaped to Persia, the land of the enemy, this army commander became Pharaoh under the name of Nectanebo II. He was to be the last Egyptian-born Pharaoh and the last Egyptian to govern his country for more than two thousand years.

PART TWO

The will of the gods

NECTANEBO CAST HIS EYES round the walls of the temple. On each side prayers and other holy writings had been carved in hieroglyphs. His eyes settled on the words that had been spoken since ancient times when a king was laid to rest: 'Rouse yourself, O King. Go so that you may govern the mounds of Seth. Go so that you may govern the mounds of Osiris.'

Nectanebo thought about his own time as king. He had 'roused' himself, as the ancient words had asked. When his uncle Teos had fled to Persia, Nectanebo had taken over the government from him, just as Horus had taken control from Seth. The gods could have asked no more from him. Nectanebo had followed their commands and obeyed their wishes. If the Persian army had broken through the frontier and was now flooding into Egypt, it must be because the gods wished this to happen, he thought. It was the same as the yearly flooding of the Nile. The waters rose and spread over the land because the gods wished it.

The gods of Egypt were important to every Egyptian Pharaoh because every Pharaoh was like a living god on earth. But to Nectanebo, the last of the Egyptian Pharaohs, paying respect to the gods was more important than ever. With foreign armies threatening the country and with settlers arriving from other lands to make their home in Egypt, Nectanebo knew that the best way to protect Egypt and the Egyptian way of life was to work hard to remind people of Egypt's glorious history and tradition. This reached further back in time than the known history of any of Egypt's neighbours. Travellers to the country marvelled when they saw the temples and pyramids, the tombs and royal palaces which had been built thousands of years before. No other country they knew of had sites as magnificent or as old as these. They made Egypt special. Nectanebo understood this, and when he became Pharaoh he devoted his reign to preserving ancient temples and tombs as well as creating new ones in honour of the gods. Throughout the country, up and down the Nile, he had ordered work to repair many of the oldest religious buildings as well as founding new ones like the magnificent temple at Edfu.

A Pharaoh's magic

NECTANEBO HAD DONE SOMETHING ELSE AS WELL. Like every Pharaoh before him, he had used magic. In the past some Pharaohs may not have paid as much attention to the gods as Nectanebo, but now that the gods and their traditions were helping to preserve the country, Nectanebo made use of all the arts and skills of his predecessors, and one of these was magic.

For the Egyptians of Nectanebo's day magic was not an entertainment. It was something serious and powerful. Only a few people understood it and knew how to use it. For the magic they practised was a way of communicating directly with the gods and winning their approval.

As he stood alone in the temple of Horus, Nectanebo was surrounded by magic. The hieroglyphs on the walls contained magic spells that the gods would understand. When the body of someone who had died was being prepared for burial, the priests working on the body used to recite special prayers that would help bring the dead person back to life in the next world. When they were preparing the mummy of a dead king, their magic spells would help the king come to life as a god and take his place in the heavens alongside the other gods.

However, Nectanebo knew that magic could be used to protect his people in other ways. During his reign so-called healing statues were common throughout Egypt. These were effigies of priests or other holy men decorated with hieroglyphic spells that were believed to cure illnesses. Many of these statues had basins in which holy water was poured. Anyone who drank this water would absorb the power of the magic in the statue, and this might lead to a cure.

The healing statues were popular and many people believed in the powers they brought from the gods. The belief in them extended to other stones decorated with hieroglyphs which spread throughout Egypt at this time. These stones, which looked like boundary markers, were often made from a special green or grey stone that the Egyptians believed had special powers. They were all dedicated to the god Horus, and because Nectanebo the Falcon was closely associated with Horus, people began to connect the power of these magic stones with their Pharaoh.

The magic works

THE HORUS STONES described the god's victory over snakes, scorpions and demons. People saw that Horus had conquered evils in the other world and they understood that Nectanebo, the servant of Horus on earth, could overcome everything that threatened their land. All over Egypt people saw the victories of Horus in the magic stones and they took heart from knowing that their Pharaoh could use the same magic to protect them.

Proof of the power of the Pharaoh's magic came in the year 351BC when the Persians gathered on the north-east frontier of Egypt and launched an attack. This turned out to be a disaster for the invading army. Worse was to follow for the Persians. When the people of the Persian provinces close to Egypt saw how badly the invasion had failed, they rose up in revolt. So instead of conquering Egypt, the Persians found themselves having to put down a rebellion in countries they thought they already controlled. News of the Persian disaster spread through Egypt, showing that faith in the gods and Egyptian tradition had been rewarded. For this they had the Pharaoh to thank – and his secret magic.

PART THREE

A changing world

NECTENEBO WONDERED how the people would react to the news of the invasion. Would they still have faith in his magic? The Persian invasion had failed only eight years earlier. Nectanebo had trained as a soldier, but since becoming Pharaoh he had acted more like a high priest than a general. Surely he couldn't have been wrong in doing this? Showing honour to the gods, preserving the ancient traditions of Egypt were just as important as protecting the land from invaders, weren't they?

As he stood before the statue of Horus, Nectanebo was confused. To his people he and the god were one and the same. Horus reigned in the heavens while Nectanebo reigned on earth. They communicated through magic and until now, until the news from the frontier had arrived, they had succeeded and been victorious.

But the world was changing. When Nectanebo looked back down the long line of Pharaohs who had ruled before him, he knew that the world in which they had reigned was very different. Egypt had been powerful then. Once it had been the most powerful country in the ancient world. Now other empires, other countries, had grown powerful, more powerful even than Egypt. Persia had a mighty empire that stretched eastwards from the great sea of Syria. Closer to home were the small city-states of Greece. Nectanebo could see that they too would conquer lands and become as powerful as Persia, as powerful as Egypt had once been.

Pharaoh's spell

'LIFT UP YOUR FACES, you gods who are in the netherworld, for the king has come so that you may see him, he having become the great god.' Nectanebo repeated this spell quietly to himself. It was spoken by funeral priests when the soul of a dead king passed into the next world and took its place among the gods. Would anyone say this prayer for him, he wondered. A magnificent sarcophagus had already been prepared for his burial. Nectanebo hoped he would live for many years to come, but like every Pharaoh before him it was his duty to make proper preparations for his passing into the next world. Would this still happen now, he asked himself. Would he ever be buried in his fine sarcophagus and laid to rest in his splendid tomb? He knew that the Persian army invading Egypt was big and well armed. For every Egyptian soldier defending the country, there were three Persian soldiers eager to conquer it. As a soldier himself, Nectanebo knew that this time the Persians would win. As a king, he had to decide which was the best way for him to serve his country.

A time to choose

SHOULD THE PHARAOH STAY AND FIGHT and die at the head of his troops? History might look on him as a martyr if he did this – Nectanebo the Falcon, who sacrificed his own life for his kingdom. But what good would this do? It would not stop the Persians from conquering Egypt. What was the best thing Nectanebo could do? Perhaps it would be better to escape with his son, the prince and future Pharaoh, and the rest of his family. In time the Persian occupation of Egypt might begin to grow weak. If Nectanebo or his son were safe, even if this meant escaping to another country, they might be able to lead the Egyptian people against the Persians and win Egypt its freedom once again. Is this not what the gods would want? Would this not continue Egypt's long history?

Thoughts like this kept swinging one way and then the other in Nectanebo's mind, like a door banging in the wind. At the same time he could picture the Persian army marching steadily onwards – marching closer and closer as every hour passed. Nectanebo had once commanded a large army. He could imagine the sight of this Persian army: mile after mile of tramping men carrying spears and shields, swords and armour, and pack animals laden with tents and food and the soldiers' belongings. Tens of thousands of feet and hooves would be throwing up a huge cloud of dust. This would be the first anyone would see of the army as it approached – a cloud darkening the sky. It was a terrifying sight, and Nectanebo knew that now there was nothing that he or his generals, or the soldiers left to defend the city, could do to stop the advancing Persians.

PART FOUR

A message from Horus

PERHAPS HORUS WOULD GUIDE HIM? Nectanebo knelt down in front of the statue and stretched his hands towards the falcon head of the god as if he was reaching for something that the god was offering to him. He closed his eyes to concentrate on the message that Horus might be sending in reply.

When he opened his eyes after a few moments, Nectanebo felt as if his gaze was being led to a particular part of the temple. He let his eyes follow and then stop when they caught sight of another magic spell carved on the wall. He read what it said: 'Fear and tremble, you violent ones who are in the storm clouds of the sky. He split open the earth by means of what he knew on the day when he wished to come there.'

Was this a message from Horus? Nectanebo looked again at the hieroglyphs. 'You violent ones who are in the storm clouds of the sky.' These words normally referred to the gods, but in Nectanebo's imagination they could also be the Persians, the violent warriors who were covering Egypt with the 'storm clouds' of their invasion.

But who was the mysterious man in the second part of the spell? Nectanebo could not be certain. The words were usually used to describe a king who had gone to heaven and become a victorious god. Could this be Nectanebo himself? He did not think so. How could he become victorious against the Persians? It might be his son, however. If Nectanebo carried him to safety, maybe in time he would return to defeat the Persians, to 'split open the earth' in the words of the spell.

It did seem that Horus was honouring his faithful worshipper in his hour of need. If nothing else, the magic spell had helped Nectanebo decide what he should do.

Obeying the god

BOWING TO THE STATUE OF THE FALCON-HEADED GOD for the last time, Nectanebo strode to the doors of the temple, drew them open and called for his chamberlain.

This time the man came running and arrived with a worried look on his face.

'Go to the queen,' Nectanebo commanded. 'Tell her to prepare the royal family for a journey. We must leave very soon. You must come as well, so send word to your family that a royal escort will bring them to safety with us.'

The worry on the chamberlain's face changed to a look of relief. 'Thank you, your Highness,' he said, 'thank you.'

'Are the generals and chief priests coming to the council chamber?'

'All will be there at noon, when Amun Re reaches the highest point of the day.'

'Good,' replied Nectanebo, 'for I have a message from the great god Horus that every one of them must hear.'

With these words Nectanebo dismissed the chamberlain and made his way to the council chamber where he would address the generals and the chief priests, and reveal to them the message that the magic of Nectanebo the Falcon had brought from the god.

Stories and legends

WHAT HAPPENED AT THAT MEETING and what happened afterwards is not recorded. It is not certain to which country Nectanebo II travelled when he left Egypt for the last time. Some legends speak of him journeying to Ethiopia, the mountainous country in the north-east corner of Africa where one of the branches of the river Nile begins its long journey northwards to the sea. Other legends tell how Nectanebo settled in Macedonia in northern Greece. However, the legends do agree on one detail of his life – even after leaving Egypt and losing his kingdom, Nectanebo still practised his magic.

A statue of Nectanebo's son has been found, but he does not appear to have been an effective ruler of Egypt, because not even his name has been recorded. That is why Nectanebo became the last Egyptian-born Pharaoh.

However, the magic prophesy from Horus may not have been wrong. Although Nectanebo's son did not overthrow the Persian invaders and win back the land of Egypt from them, another man did succeed in doing this not many years later. He was a Greek king called Alexander the Great and he came from the kingdom of Macedonia, the same mountainous kingdom in northern Greece where one of the legends tells of Nectanebo finding his final resting place.

Stories of Egyptian magic have lasted to this day – one of the most popular of them is the story of the 'Sorcerer's Apprentice'. So maybe in some magical way Nectanebo did play his part in defeating the Persian invaders after all.

But that remains one of the fascinations of every kind of magic – doesn't it? You can never really know how a work of magic will turn out or, what will happen when it does.